Inspiring | Educating | Creating | Entertaining

Brimming with creative inspiration, how-to projects, and useful information to enrich your everyday life, quarto.com is a favorite destination for those pursuing their interests and passions.

This edition published in 2022 by Chartwell Books, an imprint of The Quarto Group
142 West 36th Street, 4th Floor
New York, NY 10018 USA
T (212) 779-4972 F (212) 779-6058
www.Quarto.com

First published in 2021 by Wide Eyed Editions, an imprint of The Quarto Group
The Old Brewery, 6 Blundell Street, London N7 9BH, United Kingdom.
T (0)20 7700 6700 F (0)20 7700 8066 www.Quarto.com

10 9 8 7 6 5 4 3 2 1

Chartwell titles are also available at discount for retail, wholesale, promotional, and bulk purchase. For details, contact the Special Sales Manager by email at specialsales@quarto.com or by mail at The Quarto Group, Attn: Special Sales Manager, 100 Cummings Center Suite 265D, Beverly, MA 01915, USA.

ISBN: 978-0-7858-4149-4

Published by Georgia Amson-Bradshaw
Designed by Picnic Design
Commissioned and edited by Lucy Brownridge
Production by Dawn Cameron

Printed in China

LORE
OF THE
WILD

FOLKLORE & WISDOM FROM NATURE

CLAIRE COCK-STARKEY

ILLUSTRATED BY AITCH

chartwell
books

CONTENTS

ANIMALS

BIRDS

BUGS

FLOWERS, PLANTS, AND TREES

WEATHER LORE

OMENS

THE FAITHFUL HOUND GELERT

a Welsh legend

Welsh prince Llewellyn the Great lived in a grand palace in the heart of Snowdonia in what today is known as Beddgelert. He loved to hunt and spent many a happy day out in the forests with his pack of hounds. But one day, when he called his dogs to him, his favorite hound Gelert did not appear. Keen to get going, Llewellyn shrugged his shoulders and set off without his faithful friend.

When Llewellyn returned from the hunt he was relieved to see Gelert bounding joyfully towards him. But his happiness soon melted away when he noticed that his dog's muzzle was dripping with blood. Panic-stricken, Llewellyn raced upstairs to his baby son's room and was horrified to discover the cradle upturned on the floor, blood spatters up the wall and no sign of his son. How could his favorite dog kill his precious son? Wild and stricken with grief Llewellyn plunged his sword into Gelert.

As the dog died he let out a woeful yowl pierced only by the sound of a baby crying. It couldn't be! Llewellyn rushed over to where the sound seemed to come from, beneath the upturned cradle. There he found his son and heir, smiling up at him. Lying beside the child was the body of an enormous wolf covered in blood. Letting out a cry of anguish as he hugged his baby to his chest, Llewellyn realized his mistake too late.

His faithful Gelert had not harmed his baby boy but had been protecting him from the wolf. Llewellyn picked up the limp body of his dog, carried him out of the gates of his palace and buried him under a large pile of rocks so all could see the resting place of this most brave of animals. The grave served as a reminder that we must not be so quick to jump to conclusions and a memorial to the devotion and courage of dogs. Although Gelert could never be replaced, from then on Llewellyn always kept a pack of hounds to guard his precious family.

The village of Beddgelert (meaning "grave of Gelert" in Welsh) was named in his honor some years later and today many people flock to visit the grave of the great dog. The grave itself is not old enough to be the actual resting place of Gelert but the legend ensures that the story of this faithful hound lives on.

DOGS AND CATS

Dogs and cats have been the beloved companions of humans for hundreds of years. In many cultures faithful dogs, such as Cerberus the many-headed dog from Greek mythology, guard the gates of the underworld. Meanwhile, cats tend to be treated with suspicion. They have often been considered supernatural beings and the friends of dangerous witches.

In Germany it's bad luck for a black cat to cross your path. If this happened at the start of a journey it was thought best to go home and set off again another day.

Some say that if you look deep into a cat's eyes you will see the world of the fairies. In Celtic mythology Cat Sith (meaning fairy cat) is an enormous black cat the size of a dog with a white star on its chest. She is said to steal the souls of the dead.

In British Folklore, the Grim is a large black dog with glowing eyes. It is said that anyone who sees the Grim will die soon after. Arthur Conan Doyle based his famous Sherlock Holmes mystery, The Hound of the Baskervilles, on this legend and, in The Prisoner of Azkaban, Sirius Black is in his dog-form of the Grim when he is first seen by Harry Potter.

A folktale from the Congo in Africa tells that the dog and the jackal used to live together in the bush, but it was cold and miserable. Dog decided to go live with humans because they had warm fires and plenty of bones. This is why the jackal cries in the night, as he is calling for his old friend the dog to return.

The Welsh believed that corgis were ridden by fairies. They have markings on their fur that show where the fairy saddle sits.

Cats are terrible gossips according to folklore from the Netherlands. People are careful not to discuss their deepest, darkest secrets when a cat is in the room.

In Korean mythology, eclipses are caused by the fire dogs of the underworld, known as Bul-gae, trying to steal the moon or the sun. When the dogs try to bite the sun it burns their mouth and when they bite the moon it is too cold and so they can't hold onto either for very long. This is why eclipses are so short-lived.

FARM ANIMALS

Farm animals have been essential to humans for over ten thousand years. Their high value means that in folklore beasts such as cows, sheep, goats, and pigs are often linked to food, comfort, and security.

Surabhi is the "cow of plenty" in Hindu mythology. She is said to be the mother of all the cows and can give her owner whatever they desire.

Sheep were thought to have been present in the manger when Jesus was born. In honor of this, on Christmas Eve (as long as no humans are looking) sheep will face east, bow three times and, for one night only, will have the gift of speech.

In European folklore goats are often stubborn whereas in parts of the Middle East and Africa they are considered to have great dignity. In Norse mythology, Thor's chariot is pulled by two goats called Tanngrisnir (teeth-barer) and Tanngnjóstr (teeth-gnasher).

Black sheep are relatively rare and stand out in a flock of white sheep. This gives us the phrase "the black sheep of the family," which means the odd one out in a group.

In most of Europe, seeing a black sheep is bad luck, however, in England farmers believe that black sheep bring good luck.

The breath of a cow was thought to be soothing to those with chest complaints. People with lung problems were advised to sleep in the cattle shed amongst the cows to benefit from their healing breath.

The pig is the twelfth animal of the Chinese zodiac. The animals' order was decided by the order in which they arrived at the Jade Emperor's party. The pig overslept and was late, meaning he is last in the zodiac and forever associated with laziness.

Owing to their cloven feet, goats are often associated with the Devil. Some say that goats disappear for one hour in every twenty-four to go visit their friend the Devil to have their beards combed.

When earthquakes occur in East-Asia the children are reassured by their parents that the shaking of the ground is simply caused by the giant buffaloes, who snooze under the earth, turning in their sleep.

HORSES AND DONKEYS

Gods and goddesses often looked favorably on horses and took them as companions due to their majestic looks and graceful movements. For this reason, horseshoes are considered lucky. Donkeys, mules, and asses, however, are more often thought of as stubborn or slow-witted.

Epona was a goddess worshipped by the Celts in Gaul (modern-day France). She was seen as the protector of horses, donkeys, and mules. Epona, astride her horse, was thought to lead souls safely to the afterlife.

In Persia, the braying of a donkey was thought to sound like the yell of an evil spirit. Tying a stone to a donkey's tail was thought to prevent them from making the horrible noise. In parts of Europe, however, if the first sound you hear in the morning is the bray of a donkey it means you will have a lucky day.

The Greeks believed that Poseidon the sea god made the first white horses from sea foam. In Hindu legend the flying seven-headed horse Uchchaihshravas also emerged from the ocean.

Irish King Labhraidh Loingseach had horse's ears that he hid under his long hair. To keep his secret he only had it cut once a year and after the job was done the barber was killed. One barber escaped and whispered the secret to the nearest tree. Unfortunately for the king that tree was cut down and made into a harp. When the harp was played it sang out, "The king has horse's ears," and the truth was out.

In Ireland if a horse was found tired and covered in sweat with a tangled tail and a matted mane it was suspected of having been ridden all night by fairies. To prevent this happening iron horseshoes were hung in the stables as fairies are thought to be afraid of iron.

The Headless Mule ("mula sem cabeça") in Brazilian mythology is the ghost of a woman who was cursed to run through the countryside as a fire-spewing headless mule. She can be transformed back into a woman by the removal of her bridle.

COUNTRYSIDE ANIMALS

Hares and foxes are nocturnal, meaning they mostly come out at night. Rabbits are crepuscular, which means they are most active at twilight. This is probably why these countryside animals are linked to witches and bad luck because to see one in the day was unusual.

In Asian tradition, there is a rabbit in the moon instead of a man. If you look carefully at the shadows on the moon you can see the shape of a rabbit using a pestle and mortar. In China it's believed that the moon rabbit is making the elixir of life (a magic potion that keeps you young) for the moon goddess, Change. In Japan and Korea the moon rabbit is making rice cakes.

Witches were thought to transform into hares and so seeing one was bad luck. A sailor leaving on a journey might turn back if a hare crossed his path and a bride might cancel her wedding. A hare running through a village street was said to warn of fire.

Hares are often thought of as women in disguise. Many a tale tells of a hare with an injured leg pursued by a man into a barn but instead of finding the hare inside he finds a wounded woman in its place. Perhaps this is why hares were not traditionally eaten in Ireland as it was said eating a hare was like eating your own grandmother.

The aurora borealis, or northern lights, are known as fox fires ("revontulet") in Finland. It was believed the beautiful flashing colors were caused by a fox running through the night sky and creating sparks with its bushy tail.

Brer Rabbit (meaning brother rabbit) is a character from African-American folklore. He is a clever character who uses his wits to trick his enemies and come out on top. His stories encourage the underdog by showing that a weak, small rabbit can outsmart the bigger animals by using his brain.

Japanese foxes are known as "kitsune" and are considered intelligent, supernatural beasts. All foxes are thought to be able to transform into humans, an ability they often use to trick people. The older the kitsune the more powerful and wise they become. For every one hundred years the kitsune lives it grows another tail.

17

REPTILES

When snakes grow, they shed their skin, leaving the fresh layer underneath. It is no surprise then that snakes are often associated with transformation, healing, and immortality. Frogs and toads are also linked to transformation because their life cycle sees them turn from frog spawn to tadpole to fully grown frog or toad.

The Egyptians and the Greeks believed that snakes ate and then gave birth to themselves, making them immortal. The symbol of a snake coiled in a circle eating its own tail is known as an ouroboros and represents eternity.

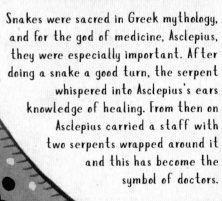

In Chinese tradition Jin Chan is an enormous bullfrog with red eyes and three legs who appears at full moon near a house or business about to receive good fortune. Statues of Jin Chan are in houses to attract money and protect wealth.

Snakes were sacred in Greek mythology, and for the god of medicine, Asclepius, they were especially important. After doing a snake a good turn, the serpent whispered into Asclepius's ears knowledge of healing. From then on Asclepius carried a staff with two serpents wrapped around it and this has become the symbol of doctors.

It was believed that snakes dare not travel through clover, so to sleep in a patch of these plants kept the traveler safe from snakebites.

In medieval times it was believed that toads had a magical stone in their heads called a toad-stone. The stones were well sought after as they were thought to be an antidote to poison. Anyone wearing a toad-stone would be warned of nearby poison by the stone heating up or changing color.

The Diegueño Indians of California said that humans gained all knowledge from an enormous snake called Umai-hulhlya-wit. The snake lived in the ocean but was tempted to live on the land in a shelter made by the people. He squeezed his body into the shelter but the people set it on fire, causing him to explode, scattering everything he knew across the earth.

Tiddalik was a frog in the legends of Indigenous Australian peoples. He drank all the water in rivers and pools until there was a drought and the plants began to die. To get Tiddalik to release all the water, the eel tied himself in knots causing the great frog to laugh. As he chuckled, the water flowed out of his mouth and the drought was over.

19

THE KING OF THE BIRDS

a Celtic folktale

Every year all the birds would gather together in a great council to discuss important matters. One year the birds noted that the humans had a king and they decided that they too should appoint a ruler. They discussed how to decide which bird should rule them.

"The strongest!" shouted one bird. "The most beautiful," called another. "The fastest," said a third. With so many suggestions it was impossible to hear any of the birds' ideas, so they asked Owl, the wisest of birds, to decide.

"Whoever can fly the highest will wear the crown," Owl decreed. The birds all flapped their wings excitedly and began taking off, flying higher and higher. But soon each grew tired and returned to earth. Just one huge bird continued up and up. It was Eagle, soaring higher than them all. "Eagle is our queen!" the birds all cried in unison.

But just then a small shape emerged from the feathers on Eagle's back. It was Wren. The clever little bird had hitched a lift on Eagle and now he launched himself, flapping his tiny wings, flying higher still.

The birds watched from the ground in confusion as Wren flew just above Eagle. Who should be crowned now? Eagle was undoubtedly the best at flying and the strongest too. After all, she not only flew a great distance but she also carried the weight of Wren on her back. However, Wren cleverly snuck a lift from Eagle, outwitting all the other birds to reach the highest point in the sky.

The two birds landed back in front of the crowd of their fellow birds with both claiming the crown. Owl stepped forwards to settle the matter. "Wren is our king because he used his brains to fly the highest." The birds cheered Owl's wise decision.

Eagle was furious with Wren for his trickery and dashed the tiny bird with her wing. Now Wren can fly no higher than a hawthorn bush, and despite being king of the birds he spends his time hiding in the hedgerows, just in case Eagle should find him again.

MAGPIES, RAVENS, AND CROWS

Magpies, ravens, and crows are all part of one of the most intelligent bird families, the corvids. In folklore they are often thought of as messengers bringing good, or bad, news. Most often corvids are associated with bad luck perhaps because of their menacing black color and their harsh cry of "caw caw."

There are many traditional ways of preventing the bad luck of seeing a single magpie. Some say you must salute and politely say,

"Good-day Mr Magpie, how's your wife?"

Others suggest you can stop the bad luck by telling the magpie where you are going.

Seeing a single magpie is considered bad luck according to the common rhyme,

"One for sorrow, two for joy,
three for a girl, four for a boy
Five for silver, six for gold,
seven for a secret never to be told."

However in China seeing a solitary magpie is lucky.

Because the magpie does not migrate it is associated with hardiness, as it can stand both the heat of summer and the cold of winter. In Korea magpies are seen as bringers of good news and happiness. They are also celebrated in France because their chattering warns villagers of approaching wolves.

22

In Norse mythology Odin, the god of wisdom, had two ravens named Muninn and Huginn. Every morning they would fly around the world and then land back on his shoulders to whisper all the news in his ear.

The Morrigan is the Celtic goddess of war and fate. She was said to disguise herself as a raven or a crow to fly over the battlefield to feast on the bodies of the dead.

Perhaps this is why a group of crows is known as a "murder of crows" and ravens as an "unkindness of ravens."

Ravens are thought to protect the British crown. Legend says that should the ravens ever leave the Tower of London then Britain will fall. Today at least six ravens are kept at the tower at all times and their wings are clipped to stop them from flying away.

Ravens are clever, and some First Nations tribes thought of them as tricksters. One story goes that an old man kept all the light of the universe hidden in a box. Raven persuaded the man to open the box, quickly grabbing the light in his beak and flying away. Eagle saw Raven and tried to take the light, causing Raven to drop some pieces, which became the moon and the stars.

SEABIRDS

Many seabirds spend their whole lives at sea and so were relatively unknown to anyone but the sailors. Sea-faring folk have a long-held respect for their feathered friends because they were believed to lead fisherman to the best catches of fish and warn sailors of dangerous storms.

An albatross has a wingspan of up to 11 feet. These big wings are hard to carry around and so the birds have a waddling clumsy walk. In Japan this has earned them the nickname "ahō-dori," meaning "stupid bird."

The souls of drowned sailors were thought to live on inside of the albatross. It was considered very bad luck to kill an albatross and any sailor who did would bring ruin to the ship.

Puffins are said to predict a coming gale at sea. If the puffins fly inland then two or three days later a large storm should be expected at sea. In Cornish legend King Arthur was reborn as a puffin after his death. He is said to reappear in feathered form at his favorite spots.

In the Pacific Islands, fishermen used to navigate by following the white tern (also known as the fairy tern). White terns seldom stray far from their home island and usually return there each night to roost.

If fishermen followed the birds out to fish in the morning and then back home again in the evening, they would not lose their way.

The Manx shearwater emits an eerie cackle at night, terrifying all who hear it. It is nicknamed "Devil Bird" and to hear its cry is a bad omen.

A legend from the Faroe Islands says that the giant Tórur gave the islanders gifts of wood, whales, and gannets on the condition that they never complain about them. The islanders soon forgot their promise and moaned about the whale, whose meat gave them tummy ache, and the wood, which was twisted and knotty, Now people never complain about gannets, to ensure they won't ever lose this valuable source of food.

When cormorants unfold their wings to dry them out, it is seen as a symbol of protection in Nordic countries. A bird seen in this posture is thought to be a warning to whoever sees it. In Ireland, seeing a cormorant perched on a church's steeple is thought to be bad luck.

BIRDS OF PREY

Birds of prey such as eagles, falcons, and hawks are often considered bird royalty, perhaps because of their noble appearance and their position at the top of the food chain. Owls have long been thought of as wise and knowledgeable. However, their bloodcurdling and stealthy nocturnal hunting patterns mean they are also associated with bad luck and death.

Jupiter was the Roman god of the sky and lightning his weapon. When preparing for battle Jupiter's companion, the eagle, would bring him his thunderbolts clasped in his claw. The image of the eagle holding lightning bolts became the symbol for the might of the Roman army.

Eagles were believed to be the only bird that could look directly into the sun. In the Middle Ages it was thought that to test the strength of their chicks, eagle mothers would force their babies to look at the sun. Any that shrank away from the sun's glare were thrown from the nest, only the bravest survived.

The indigenous Kelta people of California believe that when a tribe member dies a bird carries their soul to the next world. Hawks are believed to prey on birds carrying the souls of bad people, ensuring that only the best tribespeople make it to the spirit land.

Owls are said to be wise as they are one of the only birds with eyes on the fronts of their heads, and so they are always looking forwards.

In India it was believed that if you ate the eyeballs of an owl it would give you the ability to see at night.

The Cherokee people soaked owl feathers in water and used it to bathe their eyes to help them to stay awake all night.

It was thought to be bad luck to see the nocturnal owl during the daytime in Scotland. But Native American Tinglit warriors would run into battle hooting like owls to strike fear into their enemies.

An English folktale tells of a greedy baker's daughter who, when baking bread for the poor, used only a tiny piece of dough. However, a fairy cast a spell on the dough and it grew and grew into an enormous loaf. The girl was so surprised she let out a noise like that of an owl "HOO HOO!" and was transformed into the bird as a warning to others to be generous to the poor.

SONGBIRDS

Songbirds such as blackbirds, thrushes, and robins lend their voices to the glorious dawn chorus that wakes us up every morning. These birds are mostly associated with good fortune, kindness, and charity.

Across Britain it was thought very bad luck to kill a robin. The hand of someone who had killed a robin would always shake. If you broke a robin's egg you would soon find your own crockery broken. The warning rhyme goes,

"He who hurts robin or wren, Will never prosper, boy or men."

There are many stories of how the robin got its red breast. In Christian tradition it is said the kindly robin tried to peck away the thorns from Jesus's crown when he was dying on the cross, the blood forever staining its breast red. Another says the robin burnt its chest feathers when fanning the fire to keep the baby Jesus warm in the manger.

In Welsh tradition the robin got its red breast because of its kindly nature. The robin flew down to the poor souls stuck in the fires of Hell and fed them water it had carried in its beak. Unfortunately getting so close to the flames of Hell scorched its chest bright red.

28

Blackbirds often collect hair to furnish their nests, alongside twigs and moss. In Europe a superstition states that if a blackbird takes a strand of your hair into its nest you will then suffer from terrible headaches until the nest is destroyed.

It was thought that the local blackbirds used to be white in Italy. One winter the weather was so cold the birds were forced to seek shelter in chimneys. Ever since then they have had sooty black feathers.

In Irish tradition, the wren's especially loud song was thought to have given away the hiding place of St Stephen when he was trying to escape his enemies. As a result, St Stephen's Day (December 26) is also known as Wren Day and people dress up and try to capture a fake wren.

Irish folklore says that if the thrush built its nest near the ground then the fairies would be happy as they could enjoy its beautiful song. If, however, the thrushes built their nests high in a thorn bush then the fairies would be angry and misfortune would fall on the neighborhood.

29

FARMYARD BIRDS

In the past, many households would have kept their own hens, ducks, or geese for eggs and meat so these birds would have been a common sight. Much of the folklore relating to farmyard fowls centers on egg-laying, an act itself that appears magical!

To see a hen just as it is laying an egg is good luck, and if a hen runs into the house it means that someone will soon come to visit. A warning is given if a red hen crows, as it means there will be a fire, and if a black hen crows then something will be stolen.

The crowing of the cockerel tells us that the darkness of night has ended. This meant that people believed the sound of the "COCK-A-DOODLE-DOO" helped to scare away evil spirits that roam at night.

Across Europe a similar folktale is told of how the Devil approached a man and offered to build him a shelter in return for his soul. Just as the Devil had finished building, the man crowed like a cockerel. This caused the actual cockerel to crow in reply, long before dawn, scaring away the Devil before he could claim his payment.

In ancient Egypt it was believed that the creator of the universe took the form of a goose in order to lay an egg. Out of this egg hatched the sun. This is likely the root of the tale of the goose that laid the golden egg.

In the Middle Ages in Europe it was thought that barnacle geese hatched not from eggs but from barnacles on driftwood. Irish monks, wrongly believing that geese did not come from eggs, would eat them on fast days when traditionally no meat should be consumed.

Ducks are often portrayed as stupid in Native American lore. One tale from the Blackfeet people tells of a group of ducks who saw an old man passing and begged him to stop and sing to them. He agreed as long as they promised to dance with their eyes closed. The ducks did as he wished and carried on dancing, not realizing that one by one the old man was putting them in his cooking pot.

Ducks are associated with happiness in China and Japan. Seeing a duck flying overhead indicates that hard times will soon pass.

ANT AND BEAR

a Twana tale

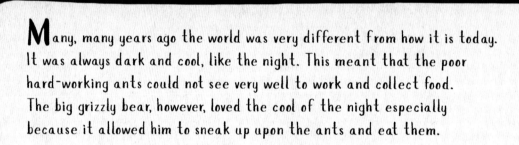

Many, many years ago the world was very different from how it is today. It was always dark and cool, like the night. This meant that the poor hard-working ants could not see very well to work and collect food. The big grizzly bear, however, loved the cool of the night especially because it allowed him to sneak up upon the ants and eat them.

Ant was tired and hungry so she traveled to the Great Creator to ask for light. Bear followed her and heard her request. Before the Great Creator could answer, Bear interrupted and asked that the world be kept in darkness. The Great Creator weighed up both requests and decided that whoever was the better dancer would get their wish.

Animals came from all over to witness the competition, bringing food and drink to share. Ant was focused on her task so she ignored the food, despite her hunger, tightening the belt around her waist to stop her tummy from rumbling. She was first to dance. As she performed a quick jig she sang, "day and light, day and light."

Bear was super confident that he was the biggest and strongest of animals. Seeing all the food laid out he greedily ate as much as he could before it was his turn to dance. Bear moved slowly and sang, "night and dark, night and dark."

The competition went on for four whole days. Each time Ant would eat just a crumb of food to keep her going and then tighten her belt further to stop herself from craving food, as she wanted to focus all her energy on her dance. Bear, in contrast, continually stuffed his face, each time dancing a little slower, until at last he was so full he fell down fast asleep.

Ant was declared the winner. But out of respect for her opponent, Bear, she asked the Great Creator to share the prize, giving her light in the daytime and Bear the dark at night-time. And that is how we came to have daylight. We know that this story is true, because when you look at Ant you can see her tiny waist, gained from always tightening her belt.

BEES, WASPS, AND HORNETS

The hard-working honeybee gives us delicious, sweet honey and pollinates the plants that grow beautiful flowers and the fruit and vegetables that feed us. No wonder they are seen in folklore as positive little creatures. Wasps and hornets, on the other hand, with their sharp stings, are less well-loved.

Across Britain and Ireland bees were considered part of the family. Whenever something important happened, such as a marriage or a death, the head of the family had to "tell the bees," of the news. If the family neglected to inform the bees, they would take offence and desert the hive, leaving the family with no honey and no bees to pollinate their crops.

Bees are easily upset so you must not quarrel or curse in front of them. They also do not like to be bought or sold. In Britain it's thought better to barter and exchange goods for them or receive them as a gift, ensuring no money need change hands.

In Celtic mythology bees are thought of as messengers of good news from the gods. If a bee flew into your house it meant a visitor would soon arrive with some good news. But if a wasp landed in your home, then it warned that an enemy would soon visit.

In ancient Greece it was thought that if a bee landed on your head, it meant you would be very successful. If a bee landed on the lips of a child then it signaled that they would grow up to be a great speaker or poet.

34

Hornets used to be feared across Europe because it was believed that seven stings from a hornet would kill a horse and three would kill a human. In fact the sting of the European hornet has less venom than bee stings, but it contains more of the chemical that makes it feel painful.

When the Greek god Zeus was a baby, his father, Cronus wanted him killed. To keep him safe, Zeus was hidden in a cave by the nymph Melissa (whose name means bee in Greek), where she fed him on goat's milk and honey. After a furious Cronus discovered what Melissa had done, he changed her into an earthworm. Zeus felt pity for his nurse and instead transformed her into a beautiful bee.

In Egyptian mythology, bees were said to hatch from the tears of the sun god Ra as they hit the hot sand of the desert.

In England it was believed that if you killed the first wasp of the season that you saw then it would ensure that you would not be stung for the entire summer.

BUTTERFLIES, MOTHS, AND DRAGONFLIES

Butterflies and moths are extraordinary creatures. They turn from caterpillars into beautiful winged bugs. For this reason they are associated with transformation. Dragonflies are also symbolic of change because they can exist on water, land, and in the air.

The humble caterpillar cocoons itself in a chrysalis and then emerges as a beautiful butterfly. For this reason, in many cultures, the butterfly is thought of as a winged soul. The caterpillar represents life on earth.

The butterfly is seen as the soul set free to fly to the next world.

Butterflies are bringers of sleep and dreams in Native American Blackfoot tradition. To help children sleep, butterfly symbols were embroidered onto blankets or clothing.

In Europe it was believed that if you saw three white butterflies together it was good luck.

36

Damselflies are known as the "Devil's knitting needle" in British folklore because of their long thin bodies. It was thought that if you fell asleep next to a stream the damselflies would sew your eyelids shut.

In Colombia, if a white moth was found in the bedroom it was treated with great respect because they were thought to be the spirit of a dead relative who had come to visit. If the moth became troublesome then it would be removed with great caution, because if it was harmed, it might return for revenge.

The dragonfly is admired for its bravery and strength in Japan because it is an excellent hunter and never gives up. Legend says that 21st Emperor Yuryaka Tenvo was bitten painfully on the arm by a horsefly while out hunting. As he tended to his throbbing wound, a dragonfly swooped down and gobbled up the horsefly, earning this bug his undying gratitude.

Snakes and dragonflies were thought to always go together in American folklore. It was said that if you saw a dragonfly, a snake was sure to be nearby.

Dragonflies were given the nickname "snake doctor" because it was believed that if a snake were cut in half, the helpful dragonfly would sew it back together.

SPIDERS

In many cultures spiders play a role in creation myths because they use their silken webs to build things. In Europe, where few spiders are venomous, they are largely seen as helpful and hardworking. However, in some countries where poisonous spiders live, they are associated with evildoing due to the threat they pose.

Little spiders of the Linyphiidae family are known as "money spiders" in Britain. Seeing one indicates good fortune and if one runs across the palm of your hand it means that you will soon come into money.

Spiders eat flies so in European folklore spiders in the house are a good thing to be left alone. This traditional rhyme serves as a reminder, "If you wish to live and thrive, let a spider run alive."

In Japan spiders are treated with caution because they are thought to be evil-beings in disguise. While everyone is awake they transform themselves into barely noticeable spiders but as soon as night falls and everyone goes to sleep they turn back into their true demon form to cause trouble.

Spiders work hard to build their webs, and they are associated with determination and effort. In France if you see a spider weaving its web in the morning it's bad luck. However, seeing a spider spinning a web in the afternoon is good luck.

38

Islamic tradition has great respect for spiders. One day when the Prophet Muhammad was being pursued by soldiers he hid in a cave. A kindly spider saw his plight and wove an enormous web over the mouth of the cave. The soldiers, noticing the web, assumed that Muhammad could not have entered the cave or the web would've broken. So they passed by, keeping Muhammad safely hidden.

In Cherokee legend, Grandmother Spider brought light to the world. Buzzard and Possum had tried and failed to capture the sun but Grandmother Spider had a plan. She made a bowl from clay and traveled to where the sun was resting, laying down a trail of silk as she went. She carefully placed the sun in her bowl and followed the silk back, journeying from east to west, bringing the sun to the people.

Anansi is a trickster character in West African tradition who takes the form of a spider. One story tells how he used his intelligence to persuade Nyame, the sky god, to gift both rain and night to humans.

39

ANTS, LADYBUGS, AND BEETLES

Ants are considered industrious and helpful because they work as a team to collect food for their colony. Ladybugs are also generally associated with luck because they eat aphids, which destroy life-giving crops.

The Myrmidons in Greek mythology were worker ants from the island of Aegina who were transformed into a soldiers by Zeus. They kept their hardworking ant character and became warriors, fighting alongside Achilles during the Trojan War.

It was believed in New England in America that ants would not cross a chalk line. To keep food free of pesky ants, people would draw around their dishes with chalk.

Ladybugs are generally thought to be lucky and so should never be harmed. If you do accidentally kill one, it should be buried and the ground stamped on three times to avert bad luck. In England if a ladybug lands on your hand you should count its spots to find out how many happy months you will have in the coming year.

If a ladybug lands on your hand you should say, "Fly away east, fly away west and show me the place where's the one I love best." The direction in which the ladybug takes off indicates where your future love lives.

An Angolan folktale tells that Dung Beetle was jealous of Butterfly because people always stopped to admire her. To make him feel better, Butterfly recommended that he impress people by becoming super strong. Dung Beetle trained hard and soon could roll an enormous ball of elephant dung along with his back legs. People stopped and marveled at the proud dung beetle rolling his ball.

The stag beetle is treated with caution in Germany as it was believed to be an instrument of the Devil. It was thought that stag beetles carried hot coals in their oversized jaws and dropped them in houses, setting them on fire.

In Japanese folklore, the giant dragon-headed beetle known as Jinshin-mushi is said to burrow under the earth, causing earthquakes.

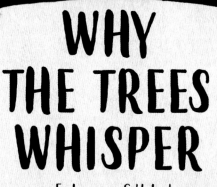

WHY THE TREES WHISPER

an Estonian folktale

When the world was quite new and animals, plants, and people had only recently been created, there lived a man called Ilmar. One morning he ventured into the forest to cut some wood to build a shelter and a fire. He spotted a tall, straight tree which looked perfect. As he lifted his axe and was about to strike the tree, it screamed out, "Please don't cut me down!" "Why ever not?" asked the man. "Because I am a pine tree and my sap can help to heal wounds," said the tree. The man stopped and considered this. Healing wounds was indeed useful. "Very well, I will spare you and find another tree," he replied.

He carried on walking and came to another large tree with ample branches that he thought would make an excellent shelter. Once again he lifted his axe but the tree called out, "Stop! Don't cut me down. I am a walnut tree and I grow tasty nuts." The man liked nuts and thought that it would be handy to have a ready supply of snacks, so he lowered his axe and walked on.

The next tree he saw had low branches and broad green leaves. He thought this tree would make excellent firewood. But again, just as he was about to starting cutting, the tree wailed, "Oh please don't cut me down. I am an oak tree and my branches protect the deer from the wind and the rain." This is another helpful tree, the man thought, I cannot cut it down.

The man kept on walking through the forest, growing weary as he went. Each tree he approached had a reason why it was especially useful and should be saved. The birch tree provided twigs to make brooms, the maple tree made sweet, delicious syrup and the flexible wood in willow branches could be woven into baskets. He began getting very frustrated but even after hours and hours of walking, every single tree, with its wailing cry, had convinced him of its worth.

In despair he shouted up to the Creator, "How can I ever make a shelter or cook my dinner if I can't gather any wood? Every time I go to cut down a tree it cries and persuades me to leave it alone."

Creator felt sorry for the man and decided to strike the trees silent so they could no longer speak. The man was very grateful and was now able to cut down any tree he desired. But the trees were unhappy at losing their voices and, if you listen very carefully, you can hear them still whispering consoling words to one another.

COMMON WEEDS

Weeds, such as daisies, dandelions, and nettles, are unwanted plants that spread naturally and cover every spare bit of land. Because they are so plentiful, weeds are abundant in folklore.

Children have long used dandelions as clocks, by picking the seed heads and blowing on them. The number of puffs it takes for all the seeds to fly off is said to reveal the hour of the day.

Borage, with its blue, star-shaped flowers, is common throughout Europe and North America. It was thought that chewing the leaves of the borage plant would give you courage. For this reason, Roman soldiers used to eat borage leaves before battle.

Never bring dandelions into the house as it was thought they'd make you wet the bed! In French, dandelions are known as "pissenlit" which translates as "wet the bed."

The thistle is the national symbol of Scotland. It was adopted after invading Norseman tried to sneak up on sleeping clansmen by removing their shoes. However, one unlucky fellow stepped on a thistle and cried out in pain, waking the Scots and saving them from attack.

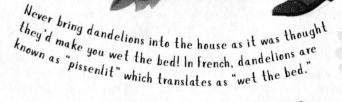

The word daisy comes from the Anglo-Saxon "daeges eage," meaning "day's eye" as the plant tends to open only in daylight. They were nicknamed "measure of love" because people used to pick the petals while chanting "loves me, loves me not" until the petals were gone and they had their answer.

Although brambles might look sharp and spiky, they were considered magical in Britain and Ireland. Walking under an arch of brambles was believed to cure any illness.

The plantain weed (not the fruit) is often found growing at the side of roads. Romans called them "planta" in Latin, meaning "the sole of the foot" as they were thought to grow where the Roman army had marched.

Ferns are ancient plants that have grown on the earth since before the dinosaurs existed. In European tradition, fern seeds collected on Midsummer's Eve can make whoever carries them invisible.

Groundsel is a common weed believed to grow where witches had walked. A groundsel plant on a thatched roof was thought to show where a witch had landed on her broomstick.

In Māori culture the spiral shape of an unfurling fern frond represents new life and fresh beginnings.

45

FLOWERS

Flowers mostly bloom in the spring and summer months, so they are associated with the hope and happiness brought by sunny days and warm weather.

Foxgloves are a beautiful but extremely poisonous plant and are said to be the favorite flower of the fairies.

In Norwegian the plant is known as the "fox-bell" and it was thought that fairies had taught foxes to ring the bell-shaped flowers to warn their fellow foxes that there were hunters in the area.

In ancient China, chrysanthemums were linked to life and vitality because they flowered in fall when other blooms were fading.

In Japan the chrysanthemum is associated with royalty and is the symbol of the Japanese emperor.

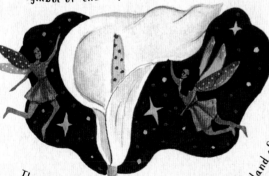

The pollen of the calla lily gives off a faint glow at dusk and for this reason they were known as "fairy lamps."

A garland of bluebells worn around the neck was thought to compel the wearer to tell the truth. In Ireland it was believed that ringing bluebells would summon fairies, and people were advised not to walk through large patches of bluebells as the bad spells in their blooms might be released.

Lily of the valley were thought to have been created by fairies hanging their drinking cups on stalks while they danced and made merry.

In a Norwegian folktales, lily of the valley was formed by the spring goddess who wished to brighten up the dark days of winter. To do so, she used lengths from her green dress to fashion stalks and dotted them with snow to create bright white flowers.

In Northern Europe roses are considered the property of fairies and so it is sensible to ask their permission before plucking one.

The rose was said to have first grown in the Garden of Eden. It was originally white but when Eve bent down to kiss it, it blushed and turned pink.

The daffodil is the only flower to grace the banks of the Styx, one of the five rivers of the underworld in Greek mythology.

In Maine in America, it was thought that if you pointed at a daffodil it would not flower. But in Wales it was believed that whoever found the first daffodil of spring would go on to find gold in the coming months.

47

CROPS, VEGETABLES, AND HERBS

Many superstitions on planting and harvesting crops developed because ensuring a plentiful crop of grains and vegetables was vital to avoid famine.

In England the time was right to plant barley when a farmer could comfortably sit on the soil with his bare buttocks. This meant the ground was warm enough for seeds to germinate.

In Greek mythology, Hades, the god of the underworld, fell in love with the lovely nymph Minthe.

Hades' wife, Persephone, became jealous and transformed her into a mint plant. However, Persephone could not remove Minthe's beautiful smell which still lingers on the herb that bears her name.

According to American Ozark folklore, corn should be planted when oak leaves are as big as squirrel's ears to ensure the best crop. But if you laugh loudly while planting corn, the kernels will come out wonky and too far apart.

Feldgeister are agricultural spirits in German folklore who live among the grain crops and take the form of various animals or birds. Feldgeister like to steal children and anyone who touches one becomes ill. At harvest time a single ear of corn was left in the field as an offering to the Feldgeister.

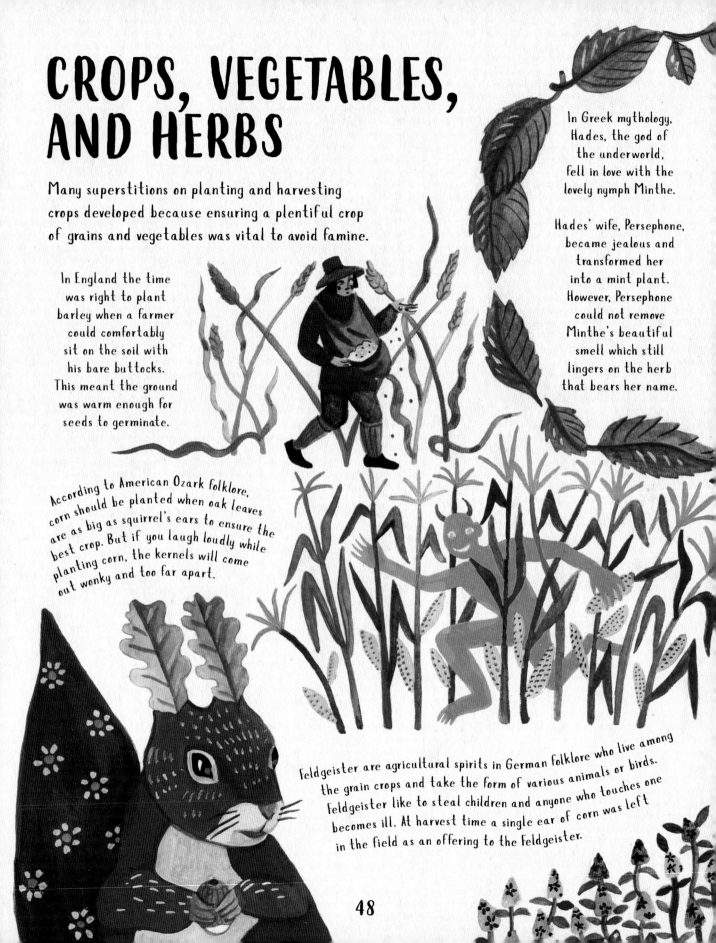

Dreaming about onions is supposed to be good luck and keeping an onion cut in half in the house was said to absorb germs.

Russians believed that pungent garlic first grew from the hoofprint formed by the Devil's left hoof and that onions sprouted from his right hoofprint.

Axomamma (meaning potato mother) was the Incan goddess of potatoes. She, alongside an especially interestingly shaped potato, would be worshipped to ensure a good harvest of this vital crop.

Parsley should not be given as a gift as it is bad luck. Those wishing to gift parsley should place it on the ground and turn their backs so the plant can be "stolen," to prevent bad fortune.

Rosemary was known as "friendship bush" in some parts of Britain and those who had one planted in their garden were guaranteed many friends. In ancient Greece students would weave sprigs of rosemary into their hair to help their memory while they were studying for exams.

Fairies were thought to make their homes in thyme bushes. In medieval England ladies gave sprigs of thyme to jousting knights as it was believed to increase strength and courage.

DECIDUOUS TREES

Deciduous trees have leaves that fall off in the fall. They mainly grow in places that have a wet and a dry season. Trees are often thought of as sacred because their branches provide shelter and their wood, fuel.

The oak tree is one of the most sacred types of tree in Europe. They were thought to offer protection as they were associated with powerful gods, including Jupiter in Roman mythology and Dagda in Irish tradition. Sick people would walk round and round an oak tree believing that their illness would seep into the tree, curing them.

A folktale from Botswana accounts for the baobab tree's strange appearance. When trees were created, God asked each animal to plant a different variety. The mean hyena was last in the queue and was given the baobab. Disgusted at being last, the hyena deliberately planted the tree upside down, which is why its branches look like roots.

Acorns will not grow on an oak tree until it is at least twenty years old and so they came to represent a long-awaited reward.

In German folklore, a man sold his soul to the Devil in exchange for money, telling him that he would repay him once he grew his first crop. To ensure he didn't have to repay the Devil quickly the man planted acorns, safe in the knowledge it would be many years until his first crop was ready.

In Norse mythology the World Tree was an ash tree known as Yggdrasil. The tree's roots started in the underworld, its branches spread out across the world and its canopy reached the Heavens, providing a vital link between the realms.

People hung willow over their windows in China to keep ghosts away. They also gave willow twigs to a loved one who was going away because "liú," the word for willow in Mandarin, is the same as the word for stay.

In Europe people planted birch trees beside their front doors because before she could enter the house a witch would have to count every leaf on the tree. This difficult task would put off all but the most determined witches from entering your home.

The hazel is the tree of knowledge in Celtic tradition. Salmon that fed on hazelnuts were thought to be exceedingly wise as a result. The number of spots on the side of a salmon supposedly show how many hazelnuts the fish has eaten.

51

EVERGREEN TREES AND SHRUBS

Trees and shrubs that have leaves all year round are known as evergreen. They are associated with hope in the winter as their green leaves remind us that spring is around the corner.

The cedar tree in Cherokee tradition houses the spirits of their ancestors. The wood of the cedar was believed to have protective properties and a branch of cedar was hung over doorways to prevent bad spirits from entering the home.

Magnolia trees were around even before bees evolved and so they are pollinated by beetles. In China, where some species of magnolia originated, they are associated with female beauty and the arrival of spring.

For the indigenous Australian peoples, the eucalyptus was an essential tree. Not only did its wood provide weapons, containers, and canoes but its sap was used to seal and heal wounds.

In China, the pine tree is known as one of the "Three Friends of Winter" alongside the plum and bamboo, because they all remain green throughout the bare winter months. For similar reasons pine trees have been used as Christmas trees in Germany since the 16th century.

Pine sap was traditionally used to treat wounds because it is naturally antibacterial. This connected the tree to healing and security.

In Finland people used to hug pine trees when they needed courage.

Ivy is often associated with love, because the plant binds trees and walls as though in an embrace.

For many Native American tribes, the fir tree is linked with protection. The Salish used fir branches to keep away evil spirits. Algonquian tribespeople placed fir and spruce needles into pillows to protect the sleeper from illness, and for the Hopi, the fir tree was once a medicine man who transformed himself into a tree.

Farmers often left holly bushes uncut in hedgerows. This was because it was thought witches liked to run along the tops of hedges and the spiky holly bush would stop them in their path.

In Wales it is unlucky to bring holly into the house before Christmas Eve as it is thought to cause family arguments.

FRUITING TREES

Trees with fruits or berries are important because they provide food for animals, birds, and humans. For this reason, they are often treated with respect to ensure they continue to be fruitful.

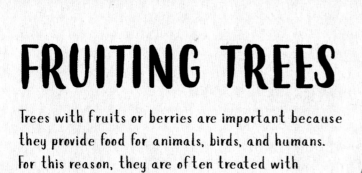

If an apple tree blossomed out of season, then it foretold misfortune. In some parts of Britain, it was considered wise to leave one apple on the tree after harvest as an offering to the pixies.

Plum trees are important in Chinese culture. Plums are linked to perseverance because they blossom in late winter, providing hope for the coming spring.

An elder tree's perfumed flowers, leaves, and berries make it an unwise choice to fall asleep under as the fragrance can cause magical, never-ending sleep.

Magic wands and musical instruments were often made from the wood of the elder tree. However, some say that if you burn elder wood in the fire you would see the Devil in the flames.

The Irish believed that the hawthorn was a fairy bush under which fairies would meet. It was very unwise to cut one down for fear of upsetting the fairies. Many roads have been diverted or building plans changed to avoid cutting down a hawthorn.

54

The blackthorn with its long spiky thorns, is known to be home to Lunantisidhe, or moon fairies, in Irish folklore. The Lunantisidhe jealously guard the tree and curse anyone who tried to pick its fruit or cut a branch. On a full moon, the fairies leave the tree to worship the moon goddess, making it the safest time to harvest its fruit.

Mulberries were once thought to be white. However, in Greek myth when doomed lovers Pyramus and Thisbe died at the foot of the mulberry tree, their blood soaked down into the roots, turning the fruit dark red.

Rowan trees grow in poor soil and craggy spaces and so are especially strong and hardy. In England, branches of rowan when woven into the roof of a house were believed to protect the household from fire.

In Japan the cherry tree is sacred. Its beautiful but short-lived blossoms remind people to cherish each passing moment.

55

HOW CLOUDS WERE INVENTED

a Greek myth

Once upon a time, the older generation of Titan gods went to war with the younger Olympian gods over who would be in charge. After ten long years, the Olympians won. The god Zeus and his two brothers drew lots to see who would rule over the sky, the oceans and the underworld. Zeus became God of the Sky. This gave him power over rain, storms, and lightning.

Lately the humans had become ungrateful and were spoiled by plentiful food and good weather. As a result, they had stopped praying to the Gods of Olympus. Zeus was displeased by this and decided humans should be punished, so he took away the rain. With no rain the land dried up, plants and crops died, and a great famine gripped the earth. At first the humans were fine as they had lots of food stored. As their supplies dwindled, they started to again pray to the gods, pleading for their help. Zeus was pleased and granted rain.

However, Prometheus, the Titan who had created mortals from clay, felt that it was unfair that the humans were not warned when the rain was coming. They had not been able to catch the useful rainwater or take cover from storms. Prometheus decided he would help the mortals, but he needed the aid of his brother, Epimetheus.

Together the two brothers came up with a clever scheme to help the humans predict rain. They caught a fine lamb and cut away its light and fluffy fleece. Whenever they saw that Zeus was about to make rain they would throw the fleece into the sky, creating white clouds and warning the mortals that rain was on the way.

Zeus was furious that the Titans were still meddling in Olympian business. He decided that Prometheus and Epimetheus should be punished. With the agreement of his fellow gods, Zeus turned Prometheus into the sun and Epimetheus into the moon. That way they could still help the humans but they were kept apart from each other and prevented from causing any more trouble. Prometheus, the sun, shines more brightly than his brother, the moon. He is fueled by anger at being kept away from his beloved people, whom he created.

SUNSHINE AND WARM DAYS

Predicting the weather is fiendishly difficult. However, people have always observed nature closely for clues. Sunshine and warm days are nearly always welcome so omens that good weather might be on its way were celebrated.

In the summer the Dog Star, also known as Sirius, is the brightest in the night sky. In ancient Rome they believed that the star's heat gave warmth to the summer months.

The hotter it gets, the more quickly crickets chirrup. In America, it was traditional to count how many times a cricket chirps in fifteen seconds then add thirty-seven to calculate the temperature in Fahrenheit.

Cats are especially good at foretelling the weather. If their whiskers stand out stiffly, good weather is expected but if they are droopy it will rain.

A red sky in the evening is thought to spell good weather on its way. A red sky in the morning means the opposite. Shepherds' dependence on the weather inspired the traditional English rhyme,

"Red sky at night, shepherd's delight.
Red sky in the morning, shepherd's warning."

In the Fens in East Anglia in England it was believed that if you saw a yellow frog jump from wet grass, the next day would be sunny.

58

If the first butterfly of the season you see is white it will be a rainy summer. If the first is dark, there will be many thunderstorms, but if it's yellow then it will be a summer full of sunshine.

Pinecones are thought to open when the weather is going to be warm and close if it's going to rain.

American Ozark folklore says that the sun will always shine on a Wednesday, even if only for a minute. If a Wednesday passes without sunshine, a storm must be on the way.

RAIN, WIND, AND THUNDERSTORMS

Farmers, sailors, and shepherds depend on the weather and so they were especially keen to learn how to predict coming rain, wind, or storms. These traditional rhymes and sayings were then passed down through generations.

In Britain it was thought that cows grazing near the gate meant that they were looking to be brought in for shelter as bad weather was coming. Cows sitting down in the fields also spelled rain.

In the Fens of East Anglia, people would open their front and back doors during a thunderstorm. This was so the storm would pass straight through the chimney and then roll out through the door.

Rabbits are thought to sit and twitch their ears in the direction from which a thunderstorm is coming.

In Europe gales are expected when a goat shakes its head so hard its ears clap together.

Some flowers, such as speedwell, close up their petals if it's going to rain. In England, if speedwell closes in the morning, it is thought to foretell rain before the evening.

In Germany nettles were burned on the fire during a thunderstorm to stop the house from being struck by lightning.

In Norse legend Thor sheltered from a thunderstorm underneath an oak tree and so placing an acorn on the windowsill protects a house from lightning.

Swallows or swifts flying low over the water, cats leaving a sunny spot to lie in a farm building, or sparrows chattering in the morning are all thought to indicate coming rain.

In China, the pheasant is called the "thunder bird" as it was believed the sound of thunder was created by the flapping of its large wings.

"Seagull, seagull sit on the sand. It's never good weather when you're on the land."

There is some truth to this traditional English rhyme-if it is choppy at sea, seagulls are likely to stay ashore.

SNOW, FROST, AND ICE

Signs of plenty such as lots of nuts and seeds on the trees are often taken as an omen that the coming winter will be harsh. It was important to be able to predict a hard winter because then extra supplies of wood and food could be put aside.

The woolly bear caterpillar is used to foretell the weather in American folklore. If its fluffy black stripes are wider than the brown, the winter will be cold. If the brown is wider, the winter will be mild.

If sheep huddle together in a group all facing one way then snow will arrive from the direction to which their backs are turned.

In English folklore, if you bang on an iron plow with a hammer and it makes a dull booming noise then snow and sleet are expected. If it produces a ringing sound, then frost and ice are more likely.

In Wales it was believed that if weeds grew tall a hard winter was on the way. This is thought to be nature's way of making sure the birds would be able to reach the seeds that grew on the weeds even if the snow was thick.

In French folklore, if onions have grown very thick skins then this was thought to show that the winter will be especially cold.

62

Cailleach is the goddess of winter in Celtic mythology. In the Isle of Man, she was said to be young for half the year (when it was summer) and then transform into a shriveled old lady during the winter months.

Yuki-onna is a Japanese snow spirit in the form of a beautiful woman with a cold, white face and she haunts the snowy mountains. She lures travelers to their deaths by making them fall asleep in the snow.

Hornets building their nests low in the trees was taken to mean that the winter would be a cold one, but if the nests are built high the winter would be mild.

THE SUN, THE MOON, AND THE STARS

The celestial bodies of the sun, the moon, and the stars dominate the sky and cast their influence over life on earth. As a result, they frequently play a role in creation stories and were often worshipped as gods.

Some believe that the Egyptian pyramids represent the rays of the sun shining down on the earth and blessing the pharaohs buried within.

In Polynesian legend the sun used to race across the sky meaning there was very little daylight and people struggled to get anything done. The hero Māui captured the sun with some rope and beat it with the magic jawbone of his ancestor until the sun agreed to slow its daily journey across the sky.

According to Chinese mythology there used to be ten suns, each of which took its turn to shine on the earth. One day they became bored and decided to all appear together. The combined heat of the ten suns burned the earth so the hunter Yi shot nine of them with his arrows, leaving just one sun to shine safely in the sky.

In the Scottish Highlands, to bring someone good luck you should walk around them three times with the course of the sun (east to west). Walking in the opposite direction to the sun's course is known as "widdershins" and causes terrible luck.

To have good fortune it was thought that any money you had in your pocket when you saw the New Moon should be carefully turned over.

Some people believe that you should not sleep with the moon shining on your face or you will have bad dreams. However, it was considered very lucky in Britain for a baby to be born with the light of the planet Venus shining in through the window.

Seeing the New Moon for the first time through a window was considered bad luck across Europe. People would deliberately go outside and look at it to make sure they did not accidentally glimpse it through a window.

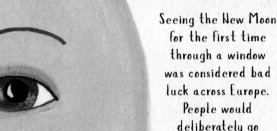

It is commonly held that when you see the first star of the night you should make a wish.

But never try to count all the stars in the sky, not only is it impossible but it is also very unlucky.

In Greek mythology Orion was a great hunter who provided meat for all the Gods of Olympus.

To impress the moon goddess, Artemis, he left huge pile of dead animals at her door. Artemis was horrified and killed Orion. Zeus then placed him in the sky as the constellation Orion to honor his hunting skills.

CLOUDS

Clouds come in all shapes and sizes, from light fluffy white clouds to large ominous dark clouds. For thousands of years people have lain on their backs and looked for shapes and stories in the clouds.

Cloud-Eater was an enormous hairy monster according to legends of the Zuni people of New Mexico. Every morning, he climbs to the top of the mountain and eats as many clouds as he can, causing droughts.

The Nephelai were beautiful young cloud nymphs in Greek mythology. They wear cloudlike dresses and carry pitchers full of water, which they pour down onto the earth as rain.

"Mackerel sky, mackerel sky— never long wet, never long dry." A mackerel sky is when the clouds resemble fish scales and this rhyme tells us to expect changeable weather when clouds like this are seen.

The Pueblo people of southwestern America believed that the clouds are the spirits of those who have died. The Cloud People live in the mountains and bring their ancestors rain.

The Muria tribe from India thought that the clouds and the earth used to be married. They were so close together that there was no space for the people, and they grew to be only very small. One day a frustrated woman pushed the clouds up and away, allowing people to grow tall.

In India it was believed that a great dragon guarded the clouds, preventing them from coming out into the sky and making rain. To end a drought, people would call and cheer for the storm god to lure the dragon away to let a few clouds escape.

Airavata is a many-headed white elephant in Hindu tradition known as "elephant of the clouds." It is said to use its trunk to suck up water from the underworld and spray it into the sky as rain.

Traditional American weather lore advises that if the sun sets shrouded in cloud then rain is expected. "When clouds appear like rocks and towers, the earth is refreshed by frequent showers."

GOOD OR BAD LUCK?

a folktale from China

Long ago there lived a wise old farmer and his beloved son. Together they worked hard, farming the land beside their rickety old shack. Their one prized possession was a beautiful white horse who helped to pull their plow and carry the things they had grown to the market. One day their horse broke free from his tumbledown stable and galloped off into the mountains.

When the villagers heard the news of the missing horse they flocked to the old man's shack and wrung their hands. "What terrible bad luck to lose your horse," they wailed. The old man shrugged. "Could be good luck, could be bad luck. We'll see," he replied and continued with his work.

A week later the white horse returned from the mountains and brought with him a valuable black mare. The old man and his son were delighted to have their horse back and soon repaired the stable and made space for the extra horse. When word reached the village the villagers once again gathered but this time to praise the old man's good luck. "What amazing luck!" they cried. "You lost one horse but now you have two fine horses." The old man responded with a wry smile and said, "Could be good luck, could be bad luck. We'll see."

The next morning the old man's son decided to try and ride the new black horse, but it was wild and fierce. It bucked and reared, tipping the boy off and breaking his leg. The villagers hurried to offer their sympathies "How awful," they chorused. "What terrible luck for your son's leg to be broken by your new horse!" The old man thanked them for their concern but replied, "Could be good luck, could be bad luck. We'll see."

Hobbling on his broken leg, the old man's son went down to the village the following day to buy some food. Just at that moment the emperor's soldiers rode into the village square and began rounding up all the young men to go to war. The old man's son, with his broken leg, was allowed to stay at home. "Thank goodness father, that I do not have to go to war," he said as he arrived home. His father hugged him tightly and said "Your accident was perhaps a blessing in disguise. But these last few weeks have taught us that not everything is always as it seems—it could be good luck, could be bad luck. We'll see."

GOOD LUCK

Traditionally people have looked to nature for good omens to inspire hope and signal good luck in the form of a welcome visitor, some extra money, a good crop, or nice weather.

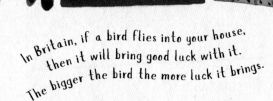

In Britain, if a bird flies into your house, then it will bring good luck with it. The bigger the bird the more luck it brings.

In Germany to see a weasel sitting on the roof of a house is good luck.

In America a cricket chirping inside the house is a good omen and in many cultures it is considered bad luck to kill a cricket in the house.

Horseshoes have long been considered lucky across Europe and North America but no one is sure why. Hanging a horseshoe in a "U" shape above a door guarantees good luck to anyone passing underneath.

In American lore if a ladybug lands on your clothes it indicates that you will soon be getting a new version of whichever item of clothing it alights on.

Dreams are often thought to contain messages. In Europe it's lucky to dream of white horses or bees. In Japan it is lucky to dream of the eggplant.

Hearing a cat sneeze in Italy is good luck. If your own pet cat sneezes then it means that money is coming your way.

However if your cat sneezes three times then it means you will also catch a cold.

The call of the first cuckoo of spring is very important. If you are ill when you first hear it, you will remain unwell for the whole year, if you are tired you will stay tired but if you are happy you will have a joyful year.

BAD LUCK

Bad omens are unwelcome and signal unfortunate things to come. Around the world, people try their best to avoid them.

Sailors once believed that if a black cat walked on board a ship and straight off again, the ship would sink on the next voyage.

Dogs often guard the underworld in mythology and so are associated with the Devil. Is unlucky for a dog to enter a church and sailors don't say the word "dog" aboard ship in case it conjures the Devil.

When you see the first robin of the year, make a wish before it flies away, or you will have bad luck all year.

In China, sharing a pear with a friend spells the end of a friendship. This is because the word for "pear" in Chinese sounds very similar to the word for "separate."

Dreaming of a hare warns of coming bad luck. In Cornwall in England seeing a white hare is especially unlucky as people who had died of a broken heart were thought to be transformed into white hares.

It is unlucky to point at the stars or moon with your fingers. In Turkey it is considered bad luck to drink water that has moonlight reflected in it.

In the Shetland Islands, seeing a rainbow is considered a bad omen.

In the Philippines people were warned against wearing red during a storm as it was believed this color attracted lightning.

In Mexico it is bad luck to sweep the house at night and in Brazil keeping a broom behind the front door encourages unwelcome visitors.

LUCKY CHARMS

Lucky charms are objects people believe can attract good luck or repel bad luck.

Actors in the theater think that wishing someone "good luck" is tempting fate. Instead they tell their fellow actors to "break a leg" in the hope that the opposite will happen.

In Celtic tradition finding a rare four-leaved clover was considered lucky. When kept in your pocket it brings good luck and allows you to see the mischief of the fairies.

It is traditional to eat carp on Christmas Eve in Poland. If you keep a few scales from the fish in your wallet you will have good fortune for a year.

Stones or pebbles with holes in them are known as "hag stones" in Britain and Ireland. They were carried to help ward off evil. A hag stone by the bed protects you from nightmares.

In Roman tradition, bay trees were planted near the home to ward off evil spirits. If a bay tree suddenly withers, bad luck is coming. If all the bay trees in the country wither, a national emergency is coming.

In 1899 a terrible shipwreck occurred off the coast of Suffolk in England. One sailor said he owed his survival to the three acorns in his pocket. The acorns were preserved in varnish and today are still carried aboard the local lifeboat for luck.

Across Europe the birch tree is considered a protector. However, if you walk underneath a birch tree it is advised to cross your fingers to prevent bad luck.

Elephants are considered especially lucky in India. A picture of an elephant with its trunk pointing upwards is said to shower you with good luck.

If lightning strikes the ground, that area is thought to be sacred and bring luck to those who visit it. But, in Britain, a lightning-struck tree should not be used for firewood, as it is terrible luck to warm yourself by a fire made from such wood.

75

GLOSSARY

Afterlife-some people believe this is the place where souls go after death.

Celtic-the ancient culture of Scotland, Wales, Ireland, Cornwall, the Isle of Man, and Brittany.

Corvid-birds in the crow family.

Curse-a spell wishing bad luck on another person.

Folklore-traditional beliefs and customs passed down in families by word of mouth.

Folktale-traditional stories passed down by word of mouth.

Foretell-to predict the future.

Indigenous-something, or someone, that exists naturally in a particular place other than from another country.

Mythology-traditional stories that are used to explain key issues, such as how the world was created.

Omen-a sign or symbol that predicts something good or bad will happen.

Sacred-something that is holy or connected with gods and goddesses.

Soul-a person's spirit. Many religions believe the soul lives on in the afterlife after death.

Tradition-the passing down of customs, knowledge, and beliefs from generation to generation.

Underworld-the supernatural world of the dead, often believed to be under the ground.

Zodiac-Astrologers use the zodiac to show how the stars and planets influence life on earth.

INDEX